MAY   2018

I WITNESS WAR

DRUG WARS

CLAUDIA MARTIN

Cavendish Square

New York

Published in 2018 by Cavendish Square Publishing, LLC
243 5th Avenue, Suite 136, New York, NY 10016

Library of Congress Cataloging-in-Publication Data

Names: Martin, Claudia.
Title: Drug wars / Claudia Martin.
Description: New York : Cavendish Square, 2018. | Series: I witness war | Includes index. | Audience: Grades 5–8.
Identifiers: ISBN 9781502632586 (library bound) | ISBN 9781502634351 (pbk.) | ISBN 9781502633286 (ebook)
Subjects: LCSH: Drug control—United States—Juvenile literature. | Drug control—United States—Juvenile literature. | Drug abuse and crime—Juvenile literature.
Classification: LCC HV5809.5 M338 2018 | DDC 363.45—dc23

Produced for Cavendish Square by Calcium
Editors: Sarah Eason and Jennifer Sanderson
Designers: Paul Myerscough and Simon Borrough
Picture Researcher: Rachel Blount

Picture credits: Cover: Wikimedia Commons: US Coast Guard photo by Petty Officer 2nd Class Sabrina Laberdesque; Inside: Shutterstock: Burlingham 23, Joseph Calev 26, ESB Professional 41, Infinity21 10, CHOI Gyoung Jun 17, A Katz 39, Olesya Kuznetsova 43, Nagel Photography 20, Andres Navia Paz 29, Photopixel 19, Daniel Prudek 5, Alexander Raths 9, Skyward Kick Productions 21, Syda Productions 4, TM_SALE 1, 15; US Coast Guard: US Coast Guard Video by Petty Officer 3rd Class Jon_Paul Rios 25; US Customs and Border Protection: 30, Donna Burton 27; Wikimedia Commons: Jeffrey Beall 44, Colombian National Police 31, ComputerJA 36, DEA 32, DVIDS 40, Michael Evans, source NARA 12, Kevin Gorman 11, Carol M. Highsmith Archive, Sgt. 1st Class Gordon Hyde 33, Immigration and Customs Enforcement 35, ISAF Headquarters Public Affairs Office 28, Library of Congress, Prints and Photographs Division 7, Orange County Archives 6, Official White House Photo by Pete Souza 38, Jason Taellious 22, The US Food and Drug Administration 13, Tulane Public Relations 42, United States Air Force 24, United States Drug Enforcement Administration 34, US National Archives and Records Administration 16, Jeff Wassmann 14, WhisperToMe 18, White House Photo Office 8, Zapata 37.

Printed in the United States of America

CONTENTS

CHAPTER 1

DECLARATION OF WAR

In June 1971, US President Richard Nixon declared a War on Drugs. Although Nixon did not use the phrase "War on Drugs," he said that drug use in the United States was "public enemy number one" and that an "offensive" must be fought against drugs. He poured money and resources into stamping out the use and supply of drugs.

A drug dealer sells illegal drugs to a user.

To understand the War on Drugs, we need to know what illegal drugs are and why they are dangerous. Drugs change the way the body works. At first, these changes may give a feeling of excitement or wellbeing, but they also cause serious **side effects** and even death. Drugs are usually addictive, which means that the user needs to take them again and again. While under the influence of drugs, users can make unhealthy choices. As a result, drugs can ruin lives, families, and communities.

Cocaine is one of the most common, and most addictive, illegal drugs. In the United States, more than 800 thousand people are addicted to cocaine. Cocaine is taken in the form of "crack" or powder cocaine. It is obtained from the leaves of the coca plant, which is grown mainly in South America. Crack is a solid form of cocaine, named for the crackling sound it makes when smoked. Taking cocaine makes the user feel powerfully "**high**," followed by a hard "comedown."

The illegal drug heroin is obtained from opium poppies.

Cocaine can cause death from a stroke or cardiac arrest. Another highly addictive drug is heroin, made from the opium poppy. Today, much opium comes from Afghanistan, in Central Asia. Heroin is often injected or smoked. It is the drug most likely to cause death by **overdosing**, usually from lack of oxygen to the brain. In the United States, more than 400 thousand people are addicted to heroin. Amphetamines, which can be powder or tablets, give feelings of excitement but can do long-lasting damage to the brain. Hallucinogens, such as MDMA and LSD, cause **hallucinations** and other changes to the way the brain perceives reality. Their side effects, including sudden death, are unpredictable. They are often taken in the form of tablets. Some amphetamines and hallucinogens are made in the United States, while others are **imported**.

Another commonly used drug is marijuana, or cannabis, from the cannabis plant. It is usually smoked, often as a "joint." Marijuana may relieve pain and relax the user, but it may also cause anxiety in some cases. These drugs are illegal, so their users, sellers (usually called dealers), **traffickers**, and growers face **prosecution** and imprisonment. Today, one exception is marijuana, which is not illegal to use in certain US states.

Some legal drugs, or medications, are also addictive. Around 1.8 million people in the United States are addicted to painkillers obtained on prescription. Another 400 thousand Americans are addicted to mood-altering drugs, such as Valium and Xanax, which are often prescribed for anxiety. However, the focus of the War on Drugs has been largely on illegal drugs.

Drugs have been used in one form or another for thousands of years. For example, the Inca chewed the leaves of the coca plant, and the ancient Greeks took opium to soothe their aches and pain. Every drug was legal until governments started to pass laws banning the use or sale of particular drugs. These laws were usually passed when a government became aware that a drug was causing social problems. Sometimes that awareness came from police or medical reports. Usually, laws were passed because of growing concern among the public that a drug was causing **antisocial** behavior.

In the 1800s, opiates (obtained from opium poppies, as in the case of heroin), cocaine, and marijuana were still legal and in fairly widespread use in the United States. Amazingly, until the 1890s, it was possible to buy cocaine through the Sears & Roebuck catalog. Until 1906, Coca-Cola contained coca leaves. However, from the 1880s, some states passed laws banning the smoking of opium in public. Opium "dens," where opium was smoked, were often run by the Chinese community, so opium addiction was mistakenly viewed as confined to that community. In fact, doctors were prescribing opiates in liquid form for women from all communities, to help with so-called "female troubles." Opium addiction was not uncommon among women. In 1909, the first US federal law banning the use of a substance was passed: the Smoking Opium Exclusion Act. Laws against cocaine and marijuana followed.

In 1932, a sheriff and his deputies pour away illegal alcohol.

The counterculture movement grew out of the Haight-Ashbury neighborhood in San Francisco.

In 1920, the manufacture and sale of another drug was banned: alcohol. Although the **prohibition** of alcohol did initially cut down the drinking of alcohol in the United States, it soon began to rise again. Prohibition also led to a growth in criminal gangs who made, imported, or sold alcohol. The tax that had previously been paid on sales of alcohol was missed by the government. In 1933, the manufacture and sale of alcohol were legalized again.

Until the 1960s, drug use was not seen as a widespread problem. As in the case of opium, the public tended to view it as limited to particular communities. However, in the 1960s, there was a sharp rise in drug use in the United States. One of the main reasons for this was the counterculture movement, which began in San Francisco, California, and spread through the country. Drug use became part of the movement's rebellion against the attitudes and rules of the older generation. It becamse fashionable to smoke marijuana. Some people wanted to "expand their minds" by using drugs such as LSD, which had been developed in 1938, and amphetamines. At the time, most people did not know what damage these drugs could do because there had been little research into their effects.

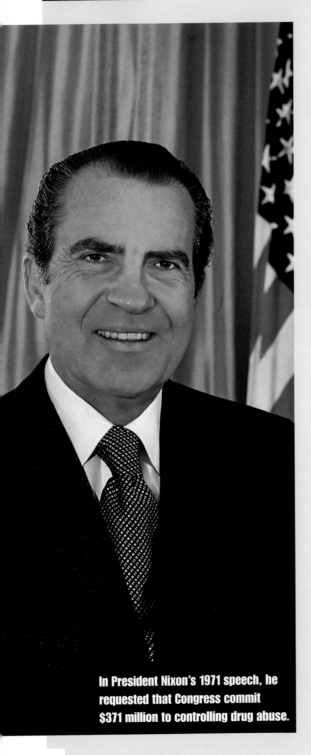

In President Nixon's 1971 speech, he requested that Congress commit $371 million to controlling drug abuse.

The older generation was deeply concerned about drug use among the young. A series of laws soon followed. In 1966, LSD was made illegal, joining older drugs on the list of banned substances. Another important law that year was the Narcotics Addict Rehabilitation Act, which gave addicts the option of treatment rather than being sent to prison. In 1970, President Nixon passed the Controlled Substance Act. It organized drugs into five "schedules," with the most addictive and dangerous drugs in schedule 1 and less harmful medications, such as cough suppressants, in schedule 5. The listed drugs became "controlled substances" with rules about their supply and use. When new drugs were developed, these could be added to the list.

On June 17, 1971, President Nixon gave a speech to Congress on "Drug Abuse Prevention and Control." He outlined changes to the law, new measures to stop the supply of drugs, and the need for treatment for addiction. After he gave a press conference about his measures, journalists started to use the phrase "War on Drugs" to describe his policy. Ever since, that phrase has been used to describe the United States' policy on drugs. That policy

From the start, the War on Drugs has been centered on making drug use a crime.

was based on laws banning the use and trade of drugs. The same policy was rolled out internationally by the **United Nations (UN)** through three **conventions** in 1961, 1971, and 1988. These conventions ban the international trade in drugs.

From the start of the War on Drugs, three methods have been used to try to solve the problem of drugs. The first is based on making drug use a crime. The idea is that if punishments are severe, people will stop using drugs. If we look at drug use as a two-part problem—supply of drugs and demand for drugs—this method aims to wipe out the demand for drugs. The second method is based on the idea that drugs

themselves are the problem because they are addictive and dangerous. It aims to stop the supply of drugs by working against traffickers and dealers. The third method is based on the idea that drug addiction is a treatable disease. This means that neither the dealer nor the user is the cause of the problem. Instead, the problem is seen as having a range of causes, from unemployment to emotional issues. This third method aims to reduce the demand for drugs by treating addiction rather than punishing users. Over the course of the War on Drugs, sometimes one of these three methods has been heavily focused on, while at other times, a combination of them has been tried.

Nixon tried to fight his war on both the supply and demand fronts. Much of the money he requested was put into stopping the supply of drugs from coming into the country, particularly from Mexico. Nixon announced Operation Intercept in 1969, before his official "declaration of war" in 1971. During the operation, border controls between Mexico and the United States were tightened to the extent that ordinary crops rotted at the border before they were allowed through. Due to the operation's unpopularity, it lasted only twenty days. Nixon also tried to combat the demand for drugs. He did this by enforcing tougher laws around drugs. The number of "no-knock" raids grew, in which police enter without warning the homes of those suspected of having drugs. A new federal government agency, the Drug Enforcement Administration (DEA), was created by merging existing departments that had, until then, had small budgets and staffs. The DEA has enforced drug laws at home and overseas ever since.

In addition to legal approaches, Nixon also put significant amounts of money into programs for treating drug addiction. This was the first time in US history that this had been the case. As he said in his famous 1971 speech, the root of the drug problem was the demand for drugs in the United States and that "as long as there is a demand, there will be those willing to take the risks of meeting the demand."

The DEA works with Border Patrol to prevent illegal drugs from getting into the United States.

U.S. BORDER PATROL

I WITNESS WAR

A DEA agent wears a balaclava during a raid for illegal drugs.

In his June 17, 1971, speech to Congress, President Richard Nixon spoke about the problems of drug abuse and the reasons why people may turn to drugs:

"... The threat of narcotics among our people is one which properly frightens many Americans. It comes quietly into homes and destroys children, it moves into neighborhoods and breaks the fiber of community which makes neighbors. It is a problem which demands compassion, and not simply condemnation, for those who become the victims of narcotics and dangerous drugs. We must try to better understand the confusion and disillusion and despair that bring people, particularly young people, to the use of narcotics and dangerous drugs ..."

In this sentence, what does President Nixon make drug use sound like?

What reasons does Nixon give for the demand for drugs among young people?

What can you find out about Nixon's antidrug measures, as described in the parts of his speech not quoted here?

CHAPTER 2

WAR ON DRUG USE

When Ronald Reagan became president in 1981, he stepped up the War on Drugs. His focus was on combating drug use through stronger law enforcement. President Reagan increased the amount spent on antidrug programs from $437 million to $1.4 billion per year, yet, he cut slightly the money spent on drug treatment and education.

A main reason for Reagan's focus on the War on Drugs was the "crack **epidemic**," which was seen to be a particular problem in inner-city African American communities. However, African Americans are not more likely to be drug users than any other community. According to a 2011 survey by the Substance Abuse and Mental Health Services Administration, white Americans are more likely to have tried illegal drugs than black and Hispanic Americans. However, the use of particular drugs differs between communities because of availability and cost.

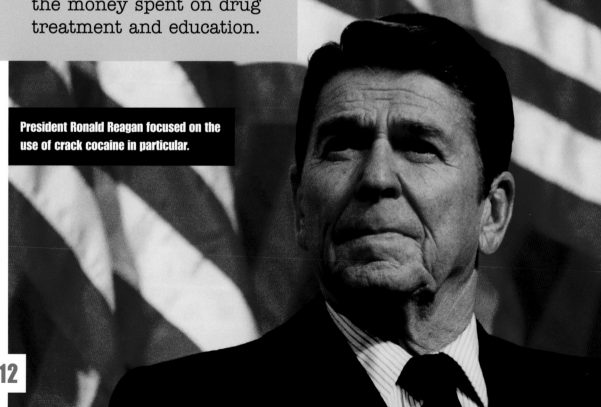

President Ronald Reagan focused on the use of crack cocaine in particular.

During the 1980s, statistics show that African Americans were more likely to be crack users than white Americans, but crack was by no means used only in the black community. However, the government and media reports spoke a great deal about the crack epidemic among African Americans, which fed the public's belief that this was where the problem of drug addiction was centered.

Crack started to appear in US cities in the early 1980s. In comparison with other "hard" drugs, crack cocaine was cheap. It was usually sold in vials costing $5 to $20, containing a pebble-sized piece of crack. In contrast, powder cocaine was often sold in amounts of around 1 gram (0.03 oz) for around $100 to $125 (worth around $300 in today's money). That made powder cocaine a fashionable choice for the wealthy, while those with little cash to spare bought crack. Crack was extremely profitable for drug dealers because it was easily and cheaply produced. To produce it, dealers mixed small amounts of powder cocaine in water and added baking soda to bump it up. Like powder cocaine, crack is highly addictive. As a result of crack manufacture, the number of cocaine users in the United States increased

This poster aimed to educate people about the dangers of crack.

by 1.6 million between 1982 and 1985. Crack is also extremely dangerous, resulting in many overdoses and side effects such as weight loss, high blood pressure, and seizures. In the United States between 1984 and 1987, emergency room visits caused by cocaine use multiplied four times over.

Although the media's tales of an epidemic were exaggerated, crack did great damage to inner-city communities. By the 1980s, industries had been moved out of the cities, causing unemployment and hopelessness for many. There was a growing gap between wealthier people in the suburbs and those in the inner cities. The government was slow to invest in education, housing, and medical and social care for inner cities. Slowly, there was a breakdown in some of the ties that held families and communities together. Although the majority of people continued to lead law-abiding lives, some people turned to crack cocaine for relief. Drug dealers saw an opportunity. They realized they could make at least $2,000 a month from making and selling crack, and often many times more if they built up a network of dealers. Crime in inner cities soared during the 1980s, largely as a result of violence between drug gangs.

When President Reagan announced that he was stepping up the War on Drugs, most Americans were glad. Like Nixon, Reagan recognized that the main problem with drugs was the continued demand for them. To reduce demand, he introduced a policy that came to be known as "**zero tolerance**." The idea of zero tolerance was to give strict punishments to people who broke drug laws, with the aim of completely wiping out drug use. Zero tolerance was put in place by passing new federal laws against drug use, as well as drug trafficking. To catch those who broke the laws, new antidrug police programs were introduced, and existing programs were expanded. More money was put into prisons to cope with the extra inmates.

By 1985, crack use was a problem in most US inner cities, including Chicago, Illinois.

Injecting drugs with a syringe is often called "shooting up."

Although Reagan's drug policy was focused on wiping out demand for drugs, he did not increase programs for treating drug addiction. The government continued to fund some drug treatment programs, but there were by no means enough programs to help the number of addicts. Reagan also did not address the social issues in inner cities that might lead to drug addiction. In fact, federal money for local governments was cut, resulting in cutbacks and closures for city schools and hospitals. A criticism of Reagan's zero tolerance policy is that, by focusing on drug use as a criminal offense, drug users were unable to get help. During the 1970s, many states had put in place laws making it a criminal offense to sell or carry a syringe, as syringes are used to inject drugs such as heroin and crack. Despite this, during the 1980s, some charities and local health officials set up syringe access programs to give drug users clean syringes for free. Without access to clean syringes and needles, desperate drug users do not stop injecting drugs. Instead, they share dirty syringes and needles. This spreads diseases such as HIV/AIDs and hepatitis. The Centers for Disease Control and Prevention (CDC) estimates that syringe access progams lower HIV infection among people who inject drugs by 80 percent. However, syringe access progams were frowned on, and often blocked, by the government for being "soft on drugs." In 1988, a ban was placed on spending federal funds on syringe access programs.

Another aspect of President Reagan's War on Drugs also focused on the demand side of the problem. His government used education programs to tell people, particularly young people, about the dangers of drugs. The DARE (Drug Abuse Resistance Education) program was started in 1983. Schoolchildren entering the program signed a pledge not to use drugs or join gangs. Over a series of lessons, often with police officers, young people were told about the dangers of drugs and alcohol. Critics of the DARE program claimed that it taught children about drugs they had never heard of and even encouraged their curiosity. Similar criticisms were made about hard-hitting TV commercials that aimed to frighten teenagers about the dangers of drugs, as these might have the wrong effect on teenagers tired of being told what to do. As a result of criticisms, DARE and other campaigns have, over the years, evolved to focus less on the dangers of drugs and more on talking with young people about issues and emotions around drug use.

One of the most famous drug education programs was called "Just Say No" and was led by Ronald Reagan's wife, Nancy.

The "Just Say No" campaign was successful in alerting children to the dangers of drugs.

The catchy **slogan** "Just Say No" aimed to teach children and teenagers to refuse drugs if they were offered them. The message was spread through schools and included a music video called "Stop the Madness" featuring celebrities such as Arnold Schwarzenneger and La Toya Jackson. The First Lady also appeared on the soap opera *Dynasty*.

Despite criticisms of 1980s government education programs, statistics suggest they may have worked. Drug use among teenagers fell during the 1980s. According to the Institute for Social Research at the University of Michigan, high school seniors using marijuana fell from 50 percent in 1978 to 12 percent in 1991.

I WITNESS WAR

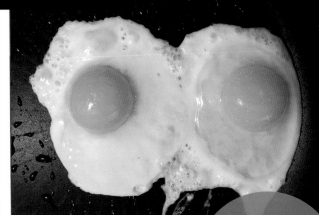

On September 14, 1986, President Ronald Reagan addressed the nation in a televised speech about the War on Drugs:

A 1980s education campaign compared the effect of drugs on the brain to the effect of heat on eggs.

"... Drugs are menacing our society. They're threatening our values and undercutting our institutions. They're killing our children. From the beginning of our administration, we've taken strong steps to do something about this horror. Tonight, I can report to you that we've made much progress. Thirty-seven Federal agencies are working together in a vigorous national effort, and by next year, our spending for drug law enforcement will have more than tripled from its 1981 levels. We have increased seizures of illegal drugs. Shortages of marijuana are now being reported. Last year alone, over 10,000 drug criminals were convicted and nearly $250 million of their **assets** seized by the DEA, the Drug Enforcement Administration ..."

What three things did President Reagan say drugs are doing to US society?

In your own words, what steps did Reagan's administration take against drugs between 1981 and 1986?

Look up the word "assets" to understand its meaning. Can you discover more about the seizure of the assets of drug criminals?

17

CHAPTER 3

PRISON

President Reagan's zero tolerance policy resulted in many more prosecutions for drug offenses. This contributed to a dramatic rise in the number of people in prison in the United States. By 1989, the United States had the highest incarceration rate (the number of people in prison) in the world.

Mississippi State Penitentiary was just one of many prisons to be expanded during the 1980s and 1990s.

In 1986, Congress passed the Anti-Drug Abuse Act. This act was at the heart of the zero tolerance policy. It gave a massive $1.7 billion to fighting the War on Drugs every year. The act also increased prison sentences for nonviolent drug offenses. Nonviolent offenses include possessing drugs "with intent to supply," meaning that the offender has enough drugs and equipment to suggest they are dealing drugs. Another nonviolent drug offense is possessing drugs "for personal use," which means the offender was caught with a relatively small amount of drugs, suggesting they were not intending to sell them. A feature of the act was that it established mandatory minimum prison terms for drug offenses. Mandatory minimum sentencing laws set rules on the shortest sentences that can be given for particular crimes. Judges are not allowed to reduce those sentences, even if they think there would be a good reason.

A main aim of the Anti-Drug Abuse Act was to toughen up sentences for drug dealers. It set minimum ten-year prison sentences for those caught in possession of large amounts of drugs, since they would be major dealers,

The penalties for possessing powder cocaine (pictured) were far less harsh than the penalties for possessing crack cocaine.

so-called "kingpin" dealers. Those in possession of smaller amounts of drugs, but still more drugs than needed for personal use, were given five-year prison sentences. These people were believed to be "midlevel" dealers. By the new laws, someone in possession of 5,000 grams (176 oz) of powder cocaine would be given a sentence of ten years. Someone with 500 grams (17 oz) of powder cocaine would get a five-year prison sentence. A major criticism of the Act was that the laws were different for crack cocaine and powder cocaine. For crack cocaine, the amounts needed to get five- and ten-year sentences were reduced to one-hundredth of the quantity. This meant that someone found in possession of 5 grams (0.17 oz) of crack was given a mandatory five-year prison sentence. The stated reasoning for this difference between types of cocaine was the severity of the crack epidemic. However, as discussed in chapter two, powder cocaine users are more likely to be white and wealthy than crack users. In the 1980s, around 80 percent of crack users and dealers were African American. As a result of the mandatory minimums, many more African Americans were imprisoned for possessing drugs than white Americans. In 1995, a Bureau of Justice Statistics report revealed that, from 1991 to 1993, 16 percent of those who sold drugs were African American, but 49 percent of those arrested for doing so were African American. According to the Sentencing Project, by 1995, nearly one out of every three African American men between twenty and twenty-nine years old was either in prison, on **probation**, or on **parole**.

To implement the tougher laws put in place by the Anti-Drug Abuse Act, many more police officers were dedicated to enforcing drug laws, and many more arrests were made for drug offenses. According to a 1989 report from the National Council on Crime and Delinquency, during the 1980s, the number of arrests for all crimes rose by 28 percent, but the number of arrests for drug offenses rose by 126 percent. The effect on the prison population was huge. In 1980, fifty thousand people were sent to prison for nonviolent drug offenses. In 1997, this figure had risen to 400 thousand people. Between 1980 and 1990, the prison population doubled. Not all of this increase can be put down to drug offenses, but changes in drug laws are a factor.

The Anti-Drug Abuse Act can be seen as setting the relationship between drugs and the law for at least the next two decades. According to a 2010 Human Rights Watch report, African Americans were still thirteen times more likely to be sent to prison for drug offenses, even though, as previously stated, African Americans are less likely to be drug users or dealers

Around 22 percent of the world's prisoners are in the United States, even though the Unites States makes up only 4.4 percent of the world's total population.

Incarceration does not only punish offenders, it also punishes their innocent children.

than white Americans. Today, more than one out of every nine arrests by state law enforcement is still for drug possession, amounting to more than 1.25 million arrests each year.

With around seven people out of every thousand in prison, the effects of the War on Drugs, along with other "tough on crime" policies, have been felt by society as a whole, but inner-city African American communities were among those that felt the effects most strongly. Today, more than 500 thousand people are in prison for a drug offense. It is estimated that 2.7 million children

in the United States have a parent in prison, a large proportion of them imprisoned for drug offenses. Children with an imprisoned parent suffer from the loss of that parent both emotionally and practically. Charities say they are also likely to suffer from bullying. All these factors may have a long-term effect on their life chances. Every year, around fourteen thousand children with an imprisoned parent enter foster care. These statistics have led many people to question whether the War on Drugs has actually worsened the lives of children in communities heavily affected by drugs.

The first organized opposition to the War on Drugs grew up in the late 1980s. Among the voices calling for change was the Drug Policy Foundation, later known as the Drug Policy Alliance. The Foundation argued that the best way to combat drug addiction was not to imprison drug users, but to offer them treatment. It argued that imprisoning people for nonviolent drug crimes might actually be increasing violent crime around drugs. The reasoning behind this is that, if possession of drugs is illegal, their sale will always be in the hands of people willing to take risks, and even commit violence, to make money out of the trade.

There is a strong link between gang violence and drugs in the United States. Street gangs had existed for around two hundred years before the War on Drugs was declared. There was a growth in street gangs after World War II (1939–1945), caused in part by factors such as unemployment. From the 1980s, many gangs became involved in selling crack as well as other drugs. Some of the money earned from crack was put into buying weapons, which were used to fight over "turf." Federal Bureau of Investigation (FBI) statistics reveal that gang-related **homicides** went up from 288 in 1985 to 1,362 in 1993. The National Youth Gang Center reports that, today, there are roughly two thousand gang-related homicides each year. Above the level of street "soldiers" who sell drugs directly to users, high-level criminals get rich from drug addiction: every year, Americans spend over $100 billion on illegal drugs.

This tag belongs to the Crips gang, which is involved in drug dealing, among other crimes.

Under mandatory minimum sentencing laws, a judge has no choice but to impose a tough penalty.

I WITNESS WAR

In 1984, Anthony Papa was sentenced to "15 to life" for delivering drugs for a friend. It was his first offense. After twelve years in prison, he was granted **clemency** and released. In 2016, he was granted a **pardon**. He has written a book called *This Side of Freedom: Life After Clemency*. He writes:

"Back then [in 1996], I was on the tail end of serving a 15-to-life sentence for passing an envelope of 4.5 ounces of cocaine to undercover officers. I was to make a fast $500 for the delivery. Being desperate, I wound up doing a stupid thing to make some fast money. I not only ruined my life, but the life of my 7-year-old daughter, Stephanie, who until this day has never recovered from the stigma generated from the crime I committed."

Find out more about what a 15-to-life sentence means. In Anthony's case, does it seem like a fair sentence?

Anthony twice uses the word "fast." Why do you think that is?

Do some research to discover more about the experiences of children like Stephanie.

23

CHAPTER 4

THE WAR OVERSEAS

Although some drugs, such as amphetamines, are made in the United States, the majority of illegal drugs sold there are grown and manufactured in other countries. For this reason, the War on Drugs has also been fought overseas. The aim of this side of the war has been to cut off the supply of drugs by preventing their manufacture, and to keep drugs from entering the United States.

Drug trafficker and Panamanian leader Manuel Noriega is arrested by the DEA.

Since 1961, the UN has banned the international trade in illegal drugs. There had been earlier international **treaties** to ban the drug trade, but the 1961 treaty was the most far-reaching, with 185 countries agreeing to its terms. Although some countries have different policies from the United States on drug use within their borders, the majority of the world's nations work together to wipe out the international trade in drugs. Particularly since 1971, the United States has played a major role in this global War on Drugs.

The DEA has been central to the United States' overseas War on Drugs. Today, the DEA employs more than ten thousand people. It also works closely with other US agencies, such as Border Patrol, which catches smugglers, and the FBI, which investigates **organized crime**. The DEA also cooperates with international agencies such as Interpol, which helps the police forces of different countries work together. The DEA has the power to conduct its own drug investigations internationally into groups, and even governments, believed to be growing or trafficking drugs.

In 2017, the DEA had eighty-six offices in sixty-two countries.

A coast guard offloads cocaine that has been seized in Miami Beach, Florida.

This is an extremely unusual situation, as each country usually has sole control of its own laws and policing. The DEA's international power effectively extends the reach of US laws to other countries. It was the 1986 Anti-Drug Abuse Act that set the scene for the DEA's far-reaching powers. The Act banned the manufacture and distribution of drugs outside the United States if these drugs were intended for **export** to the United States. With the consent of foreign governments, the DEA began to spread overseas. In some countries, the DEA works side by side with national police forces, while in others, particularly in Central and South America, the DEA has played a major, and at times, controversial role.

The first major overseas operations were directed against Mexican drug organizations. By the mid-1970s, Mexican farmers and traffickers were supplying more than 80 percent of the heroin and nearly 95 percent of the marijuana in the United States. The US government encouraged Mexico to regulate its drug growers and smugglers. The DEA was given permission to train a new wing of the Mexican police. In Operation Condor, US airplanes sprayed fields of marijuana and opium poppies with **defoliant** to destroy the crops. These policies were very effective for a while. To meet the United States' demand for drugs, however, Colombia stepped in.

Between 1993 and 1999, Colombia was the largest producer of cocaine in the world and a major exporter of heroin. In 1998, US President Bill Clinton and Colombian President Andres Pastrana Arango agreed on "Plan Colombia" to combat the cocaine industry. An important part of Plan Colombia was the **fumigation** of coca crops with defoliant. More than 500 square miles (1,300 sq km) of coca plants were destroyed in 2003 alone. Defoliant spraying has been widely criticized, as it frequently destroys legal crops by mistake, leaving farmers without an income. The chemicals are also believed to have an effect on the health of farmers.

This field of coca plants was photographed near Cuzco, in Peru.

A US Customs and Border Protection officer and sniffer dog examine vehicles crossing the border from Mexico.

In 2015, spraying with defoliant was halted in Colombia because of concerns the chemicals were causing cancer.

As part of the deal of Plan Colombia, the United States gave money to the Colombian government, which was largely spent on weapons and resources to fight a **civil war** against left-wing groups, such as FARC (Revolutionary Armed Forces of Colombia). Human rights organizations have criticized Plan Colombia for its support of the Colombian government, which has a poor human rights record. However, antidrug programs in Colombia slowly had an effect: by 2010, Colombia was producing 60 percent less cocaine than in 2000. As before, another country increased its cocaine production to meet the continuing high demand for the drug in the United States and Europe. In 2010, Peru became the world's largest producer of cocaine.

Despite the United States and the Mexican government's efforts, by 2007, it was estimated by the National Drug Intelligence Center that Mexican drug traffickers were earning up to $23 billion every year from selling illegal drugs into the United States. In 2008, the United States and Mexican governments began the Mérida Initiative. Under the agreement, the United States supports the Mexican police force and legal system with training and equipment, including dogs to sniff out drugs and weapons. Between 2008 and 2015, the United States spent $2.5 billion on the program.

Afghanistan, in Central Asia, has also been the focus of US efforts. Afghanistan has grown opium poppies, which can be made into heroin, for hundreds of years. In 2001, the United States led an invasion of Afghanistan to topple its rulers, the Taliban. The Taliban were closely linked with al-Qaeda, the terrorist group that carried out the 9/11 attacks on the United States. Soon after the invasion, US forces tried to ban the growing of opium poppies, spending many millions on the effort. However, they soon found that banning the crop made some of Afghanistan's poor farmers angry and more likely to support the Taliban. The average Afghan farmer earns around $200 a year. A poppy grower can make up to $15,000 a year. The US had to turn a blind eye to poppies, although they continued to encourage and fund the growing of other crops.

The area of Afghan land in which poppies are grown spread year by year after the invasion, and it continued to spread after US forces withdrew in 2014. Profits from opium got into the hands of the Taliban. In 2014, the UN estimated the Taliban earned more than $100 million each year from opium, which it spent on weapons to try and take back Afghanistan. Despite the United States' War on Drugs in Afghanistan, Afghan opium production has increased by around 30 percent since the US invasion. By 2016, Afghan opium was supplying 90 percent of the world's heroin.

US soldiers talk to children in an Afghan opium field in 2011.

I WITNESS WAR

A fumigation plane sprays Colombian fields with defoliant.

On January 25, 2013, a crop of pineapples was mistaken for illegal drugs by fumigation planes in the region of Putamayo, Colombia. The destroyed crop belonged to the Association of Women Pineapple Growers of Villagarzón. Their spokeswoman, Fatima Muriel, said (translated from Spanish):

"Day by day, these women have dedicated their work to the planting and cultivation of the pineapple crop. They harvest it by hand and carry it on their backs on dirt, often mud, paths, so that the fruit can be sold for one thousand pesos [$0.70] in small bags to cars that drive along the road. It is a tremendous effort that should be valued. They have nothing. The land that they cultivate is loaned to them or rented. How are they going to pay the banks their loans? How are the banks going to deal with this situation? This situation leaves us desperate."

Which words describe the nature of the women's daily work?

Do Fatima's words change any of your opinions about the War on Drugs?

Is there any information here that explains why someone might grow profitable illegal crops rather than legal ones?

CHAPTER 5

CARTELS AND MAFIA

Laws passed by the United States and UN make the international trade in drugs illegal. When a trade is illegal, as with the prohibition of alcohol in the 1920s, it is not usually wiped out entirely. Instead, it is driven underground, making it highly profitable for those willing to risk punishment. The result is that organized crime groups dominate the international drugs trade.

A stash of heroin is found hidden in a suitcase by US Customs and Border Protection.

Anyone living in a country with a climate suitable for growing bananas can grow, package, and export bananas. As a result, bananas are usually cheap to buy in corner stores. However, if the growing of bananas and trade in bananas were made illegal, most farmers would stop growing them because they would not want to risk punishment. As the crop shrank, the cost of bananas would rise if the demand for them stayed the same. To export bananas, people willing to smuggle them past customs officials would be highly paid. Some people would set up their own **supply chains** to evade customs officials entirely. The most ruthless people would become rich and powerful from controlling the banana trade. Violence would break out between rival banana exporters. When the police arrested high-level banana exporters, others would fight to take their place. This pattern can be seen time and time again with the international trade in drugs.

Pablo Escobar is probably the most famous **drug lord** who has ever lived. He was head of the Medellín Cartel, which was named after his hometown. A drug cartel is a large criminal organization that controls the production and export of illegal drugs. As in any large business, there are different levels of workers, with drug lords at the top, then their lieutenants, then hitmen and falcons (who act as eyes and ears on the street), and growers and packagers. Drug cartels sometimes come to agreements with each other to control the price of drugs and their areas of distribution.

Until the 1970s, cocaine did not appear in great quantities in the United States. Pablo Escobar is often credited with helping to popularize cocaine use in the country. By the early 1970s,

This police "mug shot" was taken of an unashamed Pablo Escobar in 1977.

Escobar's smugglers were already moving marijuana into the United States. Seeing the opportunities presented by cocaine, Escobar got his smugglers to stuff small quantities of cocaine into their suitcases. As cocaine use in the United States rose and rose, the Medillín Cartel became bigger and more powerful. The Cartel bought airplanes to transport cocaine to the United States, and it also bought an island in the Caribbean on which to refuel the planes.

At the height of Pablo Escobar's power in the mid-1980s, he controlled more than 80 percent of the cocaine exported to the United States. His personal income was estimated at $21.9 billion per year. Escobar was probably the wealthiest criminal in history, and one of the richest men in the world. He was hungry not just for money but also for power. In 1982, he was elected to Colombia's congress. This was the start of his downfall. When his drug trafficking business was revealed to the public, he was forced to resign. Escobar was furious. He was also afraid the Colombian government would allow the United States to **extradite** him to be tried for his crimes. To get what he wanted, he started a terrorist campaign against the government and people of Colombia. In 1989, for example, he is believed to have ordered the blowing up of a passenger plane, killing 110 people. In total, he is believed to have been responsible for the deaths of at least three thousand people. Escobar went into hiding and became one of the most wanted men in the world.

The growing Cali Cartel, named for the city of Cali in southern Colombia, had a more disciplined approach than Escobar. It carried

In 2008, Juan Carlos Ramírez Abadía, a leader of the Colombian Norte del Valle Cartel, was extradited to the United States.

The border between the United States (left) and Mexico (right) is a major battleground in the War on Drugs.

out less violence against ordinary civilians. It reinvested its profits in legal businesses. The Cali Cartel decided it would be good for business to help the Colombian police and DEA track down Escobar. In 1993, Escobar was killed in a shoot-out with Colombian police. The Cali Cartel expanded to become the world's most powerful cartel, supplying 90 percent of the world's cocaine. It is credited with having popularized cocaine in Europe. After the arrests of high-ranking members in 1995, the Cartel was largely disbanded, and other cartels took over its business.

Mexico had been a major grower of marijuana, but as the DEA cracked down on cocaine coming from Colombia, Mexico became a big supplier of the drug and the major battleground of the War on Drugs. From the late 1980s, the Tijuana Cartel became one of the most powerful Mexican cartels, shipping marijuana, cocaine, heroin, and amphetamines to the United States. Like most cartels, the Tijuana Cartel was known for its extreme violence. For example, in 1998, an entire family of eighteen people, including children, was murdered in Ensenada, Mexico.

By the beginning of the twenty-first century, the Sinaloa Cartel had become the most powerful cartel in Mexico and the world, supplying the majority of all illegal drugs in the United States. The Sinaloa Cartel is known for its use of tunnels to smuggle drugs into the United States. In 1989, the Cartel built the first cross-border *narcotúnel* (tunnel for smuggling drugs). Since then, Mexican and US law enforcement have discovered more than 180 tunnels beneath the United States–Mexico border. However, not all of them belonged to the Sinaloa Cartel. The Cartel's tunnels, nicknamed "supertunnels" by the DEA, take months to build and probably cost at least $1 million each.

Until 2016, the leader of the Sinaloa Cartel was Joaquin "Chapo" Guzman-Loera. "Chapo" means "shorty." Under his rule, the Sinaloa Cartel was known for terrible violence and kidnappings, particularly in the city of Ciudad Juarez, as it drove out its rivals in the Juarez Cartel. Between 2008 and 2012, the city was known as the homicide capital of the world, with up to twenty homicides per day. By 2014, Guzman-Loera had exported more drugs to the United States than anyone else: more than 500 tons (450 t) of cocaine alone. The DEA offered a $5 million reward for information leading to Guzman-Loera's capture. Mexican authorities arrested him in February 2014. However, in July 2015, he escaped from prison. Unsurprisingly, he made his escape through a tunnel. He was recaptured after a shoot-out on January 8, 2016.

Sinaloa tunnels go as deep as 70 feet (20 m). Some of these supertunnels even have elevators.

Tunnel Entrance

Border Fence

United States

V & F Distributors Warehouse (Tunnel Exit)

I WITNESS WAR

Joaquin Guzman-Loera arrives in New York City for a court appearance under heavy police escort.

On January 8, 2016, the DEA issued a statement about the recapture of Guzman-Loera:

"The capture of Joaquin 'Chapo' Guzman-Loera is a victory for the rule of law and the Mexican people and government. The arrest is a significant achievement in our shared fight against transnational organized crime, violence, and drug trafficking. It is further evidence of our two countries' resolve to ensure justice is served for families who have been plagued by Guzman-Loera's ruthless acts of violence. The DEA and Mexico have a strong partnership, and we will continue to support Mexico in its efforts to improve security for its citizens, and continue to work together to respond to the evolving threats posed by transnational criminal organizations."

What words and phrases are used to express the close relationship between the DEA and Mexico?

The statement rightly links Guzman-Loera to "crime" and "violence." In contrast, what are the DEA and Mexican government linked with?

Can you find out more about other "transnational criminal organizations"?

In 2006, the Mexican government stepped up its efforts to destroy drug cartels and stop drug-related violence. Violence between cartels, and against those who opposed them, had grown beyond all control. The Mexican president, Felipe Calderón, sent 6,500 soldiers to the state of Michoacán to stop drug violence there. This can be seen as the first battle in a war between the Mexican government and cartels, often called the Mexican Drug War, even though the fighting is not continual. As time passed, Calderón increased the number of soldiers battling the cartels to forty-five thousand, alongside thousands of police officers. The war is partly financed by the United States' Mérida Initiative.

By 2006, the cartels had control over large territories in Mexico and had heavy influence on Mexican politics. Their money has bought them powerful weapons, including guns, grenade launchers, drones, and bombs. Kidnappings, intimidation, and attacks, such as the throwing of grenades into a crowded plaza in Morelia in 2008, kept most people from standing up to the cartels. An estimate of the dead in the Mexican Drug War between 2006 and 2013 is 120 thousand people, with another

In 2012, the Mexican Army raids a house believed to belong to a cartel member.

Mexicans march through Mexico City to protest against drug violence, in 2011.

27 thousand missing. Those deaths included Mexican soldiers, cartel members, and many civilians. At least one thousand of those dead were children. This death toll includes everyone killed by drug violence in Mexico, not only in direct battles between the Mexican military and cartels. The violence is ongoing.

While much of the United States' cocaine and heroin arrives from Central and South America, most of its MDMA arrives from Western Europe. The organized crime groups in this case are often based in Russia or Western Europe. Heroin arriving from Asia is often the work of Chinese and African gangs. The Italian Mafia ("mafia" is the name given to organized crime in Italy) collaborates with the Italian-American Mafia and other groups to trade in illegal drugs. The 'Ndrangheta is an organized crime network based in Calabria in southern Italy. It works closely with Colombian cartels to traffic drugs to the United States and Europe. Although not all its money comes from drug trafficking, the 'Ndrangheta is probably the wealthiest criminal organization in Europe, if not the world, with a fortune of around $60 billion.

CHAPTER 6

FUTURE SOLUTIONS

By the twenty-first century, many Americans were asking whether the War on Drugs had been effective. Some were questioning how much harder the war had hit African American than white communities. Some wondered if the War on Drugs might actually contribute to drug-related violence at home and abroad.

When Barack Obama became president in 2009, drug policy had progressed a little since the presidency of Ronald Reagan. By this time, the government was spending a large part of its antidrug budget on addiction treatment programs. That amount continued to rise during Obama's presidency, although there were still not enough publicly funded treatment programs to help the number of addicts. In 2013, the National Institute on Drug Abuse estimated that 22.7 million Americans needed treatment for a drug or alcohol problem, but only about 2.5 million people received treatment at a special facility. In 2016, President Obama signed the Comprehensive Addiction and Recovery Act. This authorized

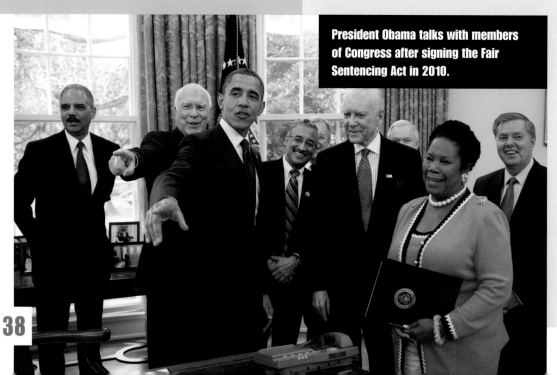

President Obama talks with members of Congress after signing the Fair Sentencing Act in 2010.

In 2015, marchers in New York City protest in favor of legalizing marijuana.

money for treatment and education, and expanded resources needed to treat addicts in prison. Also in 2016, President Obama overturned the ban on federal funding for syringe access programs.

An important reform during the Obama presidency was the Fair Sentencing Act of 2010. This reduced the difference between mandatory sentences handed out for possessing powder cocaine and crack cocaine. The difference in quantities between the two forms of cocaine had been one hundred to one. The difference was reduced to eighteen to one. This means that a powder cocaine user has to be in possession of eighteen times more cocaine than a crack user to receive the same sentence. In 2004, Obama

had described the War on Drugs as an "utter failure." However, he did not make any further changes to US drug laws. When Donald Trump entered the White House in 2017, the United States was maintaining its approach to the drug problem, banning the use, sale, distribution, and production of drugs.

Although federal law remained largely unchanged, state law was changing on the issue of marijuana. By 2017, twenty-eight states and the District of Columbia allowed marijuana for medical use. Twenty states had also decriminalized marijuana by removing criminal penalties for possessing small amounts for personal use. In part, these changes happened because some think that marijuana can offer pain relief to those suffering from certain illnesses, although its safety and usefulness have not been proven. Others argued for changes to the law to free up police resources. It does not seem as though laws surrounding the use of marijuana have had much effect on the amount of marijuana smoked. For example, a survey by the Colorado Department of Public Health and Environment found no increase in marijuana use after the state's voters decriminalized marijuana in 2012.

How successful has the War on Drugs been? What affect has the war had on drug use and on society? By 2017, the United States' yearly spend on the War on Drugs was around $51 billion. Every year, there were 1.4 million arrests for drug offenses. More than four out of five of those arrests were for possession of drugs, not for selling or trafficking drugs. Around 2.2 million people were in federal or state prison, or a county or city jail. The Bureau of Prisons says that just less than half of inmates in federal prisons are serving time for drug offenses. The Bureau of Justice says 16 percent of inmates in state prisons have a drug crime as their most serious offense.

It is estimated that every year, drug use and addiction costs the United States more than $600 billion. These costs include crime, enforcing drug laws, and keeping those convicted of drug offenses in prison. Around $12.6 billion a year is spent on housing and caring for those prisoners. More money is spent on building and maintaining prisons than on schools.

In 2013, a survey by the National Institute on Drug Abuse estimated that 24.6 million people in the United States had used an illegal drug in the last month. That was 9.4 percent of the population twelve years old and over. In 1979, 14 percent of the population age twelve or over had used an illegal drug in the past month. This suggests that the War on Drugs has, to some extent, reduced the number of drug users. However, statistics from the Department of Health and Human Services tell us that the

In 2016, the US Coast Guard seized cocaine worth $5.6 billion, which was the largest amount ever seized by the service in a single year.

In the United States, each year, around one million people have to visit an emergency room after taking illegal drugs.

percentage of drug addicts in the US population has stayed roughly steady since 1970: around 1 to 1.5 percent. This suggests that the methods of the War on Drugs have not had an effect on the number of people whose lives are harmed by addiction, even if they have cut drug use overall. On the positive side, the United States does now have 14,500 drug treatment facilities, which help addicts win their own War on Drugs every day.

Since the start of the War on Drugs, drugs have overtaken alcohol and traffic accidents to become the leading cause of accidental deaths in the United States. Between 2003 and 2013, the number of deaths from drugs doubled. Much of this increase is due to a rise in the misuse of prescription drugs rather than illegal drugs.

The prescription drugs most likely to cause death are opioid painkillers, which contain opiumlike man-made chemicals. Today, around fifty thousand people die of a drug overdose every year. Every fourteen minutes, someone in the United States dies from drug use.

Has the War on Drugs been successful in its battle against the international trade in drugs? It is estimated that around 450 tons (408 metric tonnes) of heroin are trafficked around the world every year, the majority of it today from Afghanistan and Myanmar. In 2008, 81 tons (73.5 metric tonnes) of this crop were seized, but around 369 tons (334.8 metric tonnes) found their way to drug users around the world.

If the War on Drugs has not been completely successful, what methods might be more successful at reducing drug use and addiction? Most drug policy reform organizations say that treatment for drug addiction has to be at the heart of any war on drugs. They argue that the United States should continue to expand its treatment programs, including the existing Drug Courts Program, which offers drug offenders the alternative of treatment to incarceration. Treatment for drug addiction is expensive, and a publicly funded program means that everyone has to pay for it. However, this may be money well spent. One estimate is that every dollar invested in addiction treatment programs gives a return of between $4 and $7 in reduced drug crime and police and prison costs.

Drug treatment can include medications to help addicts as they experience **withdrawal symptoms**. Treatment is also likely to include behavioral therapy. This therapy may help the addict cope with drug cravings and teach him ways to avoid drugs. People who are addicted to drugs often suffer from other health and social problems, which are usually addressed during treatment. This may mean counseling for past traumas or developing ways to improve relationships. Every addict who successfully goes through a treatment program is a major victory in the War on Drugs. Recovered addicts can go back to contributing to society by being parents, workers, and friends.

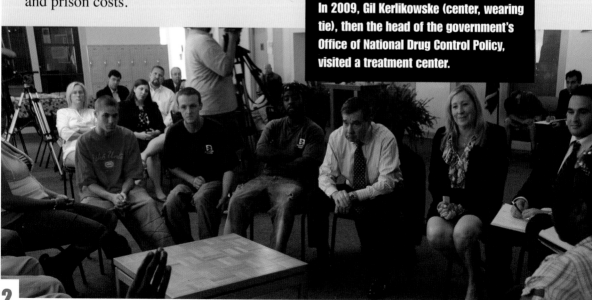

In 2009, Gil Kerlikowske (center, wearing tie), then the head of the government's Office of National Drug Control Policy, visited a treatment center.

I WITNESS WAR

Treatment can rebuild families that have been destroyed by drugs.

Sonya started taking drugs at the age of fourteen and was addicted to heroin by her late teens. She became homeless, spent time in prison, and lost contact with her little boy. Finally, she entered a treatment program. She later wrote about her recovery:

"This is a ⬚fatal disease,⬚ and it's easy to forget that. I have to treat it daily by working a program and taking action in my life to do the suggestions laid out by the program. It's been hard ... Above all else, the best thing when all's said and done—my son. My little boy. I see my little boy these days. I remember the first time I ever saw him without a drug inside me. He was six years old ... Over the past year in recovery, my son and I have begun building an open, trusting, playful, and the best bit, cuddly relationship. I came into recovery to be a mom."

What facts and figures can you find to back up Sonya's statement that drug addiction is a "fatal disease"?

Find out more about drug treatment programs in your state.

In your own words, what does Sonya feel is the best thing about her recovery?

43

The War on Drugs has been what is called a punishment-centered program, based on punishing drug users, sellers, and traffickers for breaking the law. Portugal is one country that has changed its policy from a punishment-centered program to a health-centered program. In 2001, Portuguese lawmakers decriminalized possessing small amounts of drugs. The drugs themselves are still illegal, but possessing a little for personal use does not result in a prison sentence. This is similar to the laws around marijuana in the twenty US states where marijuana use has been decriminalized. Since Portugal now approaches drug use as a health problem rather than a criminal problem, those found in possession of drugs are often referred to a treatment program.

Many people fear that the act of decriminalizing drugs will result in an increase in drug use. In Portugal, this was not the case, even though the cost of buying drugs on the street dropped. At the same time as decriminalizing drugs, Portugal invested heavily in drug education and harm reduction. Harm reduction strategies look at ways to combat the harmful effects of a behavior, rather than trying to prevent the behavior itself. In this way, Portugal invested in syringe access programs, which

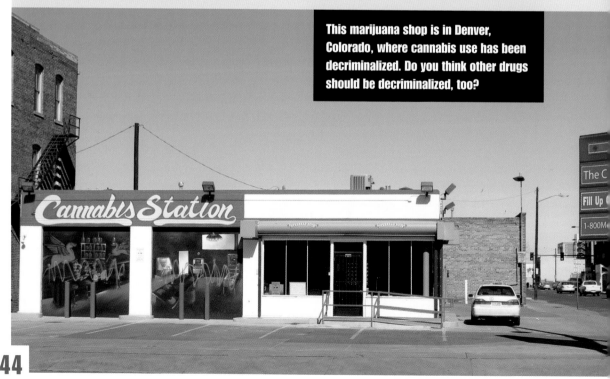

This marijuana shop is in Denver, Colorado, where cannabis use has been decriminalized. Do you think other drugs should be decriminalized, too?

led to a 17 percent drop in HIV/AIDS infection from using dirty needles. Portugal also expanded drug treatment programs. Deaths from drug use in Portugal went down following decriminalization, from 131 in 2001 to 20 in 2008.

Most people remain strongly opposed to the idea of decriminalizing the international drug trade. Who would want to see drug traffickers such as Pablo Escobar or Joaquin Guzman-Loera become rich from other people's addiction? Other people argue that a harm reduction strategy might work here, too: Organized crime groups can be prosecuted for murder, kidnapping, and intimidation, rather than drug trafficking. Some people even argue that governments themselves should oversee drug production and supply, keeping the trade out of the hands of criminals.

Since 1971, the United States has spent around $1 trillion on the War on Drugs. Was that money spent in the best way to help drug addicts and their families and the victims of drug violence? If you had $1 trillion to spend on the War on Drugs over the next forty-five years, how would you spend it?

WAR STORY

To find out more about the War on Drugs and to consider some of the issues raised by it, write your own "eyewitness" account of an aspect of the war.

1. Which aspect of the war will you write about? Perhaps you could choose the "Just Say No" education campaign, the aerial fumigation of crops in Colombia, or a day in a drug treatment program.

2. Research your chosen aspect of the War on Drugs, using books in your school and local library. With the help of an adult, you could search the web.

3. From what point of view will you write your account? You could choose a DEA agent, recovering addict, prison inmate, or civilian caught up in the Mexican Drug War.

4. What form will your account take? It could be a politician's speech (as on pages 11 and 17), a written memoir (as on pages 23 and 43), or a "spoken" firsthand account (as on page 29).

GLOSSARY

antisocial Harmful to society.

assets Property owned by a person or company.

civil war A war between organized groups in the same country.

clemency Lessening of a punishment because of the offender's good behavior.

conventions Agreements between two or more countries.

defoliant A chemical that causes the leaves to fall from plants.

drug lord A person who controls a large network of people engaged in the drug trade.

epidemic Widespread outbreak of an infectious disease.

export To send goods to another country for sale.

extradite To transfer a suspected or convicted criminal to another country.

fumigation Spraying with chemicals such as defoliants.

hallucinations Things, such as sounds and images, that seem real but do not exist.

high A short-lived feeling of excitement or wellbeing.

homicides Murders of people by other human beings.

imported Brought from another country for sale.

organized crime Criminal activities that are planned by powerful groups.

overdosing Taking a deadly quantity of a drug.

pardon When a governor or president forgives a person convicted of a crime and removes remaining punishments.

parole Release of a prisoner before the end of their sentence on the promise of good behavior.

probation A period during which a criminal must behave well to avoid being sent to prison.

prohibition Forbidding something by law, especially the manufacture and sale of alcohol in the United States between 1920 and 1933.

prosecution Formally accusing someone of committing a crime in a court of law.

side effects Harmful effects of a drug.

slogan An easy-to-remember phrase used in advertising.

supply chains The steps a business takes to get its product to the consumer.

traffickers People who trade in illegal goods.

treaties Formal agreements between countries.

United Nations (UN) International organization with 193 independent states as members.

withdrawal symptoms Unpleasant physical reactions when someone stops taking an addictive drug.

zero tolerance A policy that imposes severe penalties for a particular behavior, with no exceptions.

FURTHER READING

BOOKS

Bickerstaff, Linda. *Cocaine: Coke and the War on Drugs* (Drug Abuse and Society). New York: Rosen, 2009.

Friedman, Mark D. *Legalization of Drugs* (Hot Topics). North Mankato, MN: Heinemann-Raintree, 2011.

Gross, Frederick C. and Reeve Chace. *The Truth about Marijuana* (Drugs and Consequences). New York: Rosen, 2011.

Paris, Stephanie. *Drugs and Alcohol* (Straight Talk). New York: Time for Kids, 2012.

WEBSITES

The American Presidency Project
http://www.presidency.ucsb.edu/ws/?pid=3048
Read all of President Richard Nixon's 1971 speech about drug policy here.

Drug Policy Alliance
http://www. www.drugpolicy.org
Find out about the Drug Policy Alliance's alternative suggestions for antidrug policy on their informative website.

National Institute of Drug Abuse for Teens
https://www.teens.drugabuse.gov
Get advice and support about teenage drug use.

Phoenix House
http://www.phoenixhouse.org/news-and-views/true-stories
Learn more about drug treatment by reading the stories of those who have survived addiction on the Phoenix House website.

INDEX

Acknowledgments:
The publisher would like to thank the following people for permission to use their material:
p. 11 Richard Nixon, "Special Message to the Congress on Drug Abuse Prevention and Control," June 17, 1971, www.
presidency.ucsb.edu/ws/?pid=3048, p. 17 President Ronald Reagan addressing the nation, the White House, September
14, 1986, p. 23 Anthony Papa (author of This Side of Freedom: Life After Clemency), "What My Pardon from Governor
Andrew Cuomo Means to Me," January 3, 2017, Drug Policy Alliance, www.drugpolicy.org, p. 29 Fatima Muriel, filmed
by Nancy Sánchez, reported by Winifred Tate in "Purely Pineapples: Aerial Spraying Continues to Miss Its Target in
Colombia," March 6, 2013, Latin America Working Group, www.lawg.org, p. 35 DEA Statement on the Capture of Joaquin
"Chapo" Guzman-Loera, January 8, 2016, www.dea.gov/divisions/hq/2016/hq010816.shtml, p. 43 Sonya, "Sonya's Story,"
Action on Addiction, www.actiononaddiction.org.uk.